INSIDE THE INDUSTRY
FASHION

BY SUSAN M. FREESE

INSIDE THE INDUSTRY
FASHION

BY SUSAN M. FREESE

Content Consultant
Mariela Torres
Director of Career Development
LIM College, New York, NY

ABDO
Publishing Company

CREDITS

Published by ABDO Publishing Company, 8000 West 78th Street, Edina, Minnesota 55439. Copyright © 2011 by Abdo Consulting Group, Inc. International copyrights reserved in all countries. No part of this book may be reproduced in any form without written permission from the publisher. The Essential Library™ is a trademark and logo of ABDO Publishing Company.

Printed in the United States of America,
North Mankato, Minnesota
112010
012011

 THIS BOOK CONTAINS AT LEAST 10% RECYCLED MATERIALS.

Editor: Mari Kesselring
Copy Editor: Jennifer Joline Anderson
Interior Design and Production: Emily Love
Cover Design: Emily Love

Library of Congress Cataloging-in-Publication Data

Freese, Susan M., 1958-
 Fashion / by Susan M. Freese.
    p. cm. -- (Inside the industry)
 Includes bibliographical references and index.
 ISBN 978-1-61714-800-2
 1. Fashion--Vocational guidance--Juvenile literature. 2. Fashion design--Vocational guidance--Juvenile literature. 3. Models (Persons)--Vocational guidance--Juvenile literature. 4. Fashion photography--Vocational guidance--Juvenile literature. I. Title.
 TT507.F76 2011
 746.9'2023--dc22
                                    2010042451

TABLE OF CONTENTS

For those with an eye for style, a variety of careers are available in the fashion industry.

IS A FASHION JOB FOR YOU?

"Fashion is not something that exists in dresses only. Fashion is in the sky, in the street; fashion has to do with ideas, the way we live, what is happening."[1]
—Coco Chanel, French fashion designer, 1883–1971

French designer Coco Chanel thought that women's clothes could be both elegant and practical. When it came to fashion, her motto was "Less is more," an idea that went against typical women's styles of the 1920s. A hardworking individual, Chanel led the fashion industry for much of the twentieth century. Her styles are still popular today.

Are you like Coco Chanel? Do you have definite ideas about fashion, such as what styles, colors, and fabrics people should wear? Do you notice what people wear in fashion magazines, on television, and in movies? Do you follow trends? Are you a trendsetter yourself, choosing to wear bold new styles? If so, then you might think about a career in the fashion industry.

"LITTLE BLACK DRESS"

In 1926, Coco Chanel started one of the longest-lasting trends in women's fashion.[2] In the spring of that year, she introduced the "little black dress" as the latest style in evening wear. That dress was short, made of silk, and rather plain—completely different from women's evening fashions of the time.

Insisting that fashion should be practical, Chanel made the dress black so it would not show stains, and she made it classic and simple so it would look good on women of all shapes and sizes. The simplicity of the dress also allowed women to make it look different from one occasion to the next—for instance, by adding a scarf, gloves, jewelry, or other accessories. In addition, the simple style of the dress meant that it would not go out of fashion right away, like so many other women's clothes. Perhaps this is why the little black dress, or LBD, is still considered a basic piece of the modern woman's wardrobe.

DESIGNING CLOTHES AND MORE

Some of the most well-known people in the fashion industry are clothing designers. You have likely heard of US designers Calvin Klein, Ralph Lauren, and Donna Karan. All three became interested in fashion in their teens and began their careers working for other designers or stores. Today, they all run huge fashion businesses, earning millions of dollars a year by selling the clothes they design.

Most other clothing designers work on a much smaller scale. Some sell their original fashions in boutiques to people who are looking for something special or even one of a kind. And many more designers work for apparel manufacturers and design houses to create the everyday clothes sold in discount and department stores, through catalogs, and online. Designers may also specialize in creating a particular type of fashion, such as sports apparel or accessories.

BEHIND THE SCENES

Behind-the-scenes fashion careers involve working with clothing designers' styles and textile designers' fabrics. Pattern makers, for example, take a clothing design and create a paper pattern, or model, of all the pieces of a garment, such as collars and sleeves. A pattern allows many pieces of clothing to be made in the same design. Workers called graders adjust the patterns, making them bigger and smaller to create different sizes of clothing. Next, pattern cutters cut out pieces of fabric to be used to make the clothes. The fabric selection is done by textile buyers, who

Textile buyers select fabric to use in a particular clothing style, while textile designers design the fabric itself.

know what kinds of fabrics work well for what kinds of clothes. Finally, seamstresses and tailors sew together the pieces to make complete items of clothing.

Until the early 1900s, much of the sewing of clothes was done on an individual basis. Seamstresses and tailors operated small shops or went to people's homes to make clothes for them. Even today, some people have their clothes custom made. Other people sew their own clothes. But for the most part, people purchase their clothes at stores, through catalogs, and online. These clothes are mass-produced in factories around the world employing millions of workers. Making clothes is big business.

SELLING FASHION

Clothing can be sold wholesale or retail. Wholesale involves the selling of large quantities to stores, usually at discounted prices. Retail involves the selling of single items to individual consumers, usually at higher prices.

DESIGNING FOR THE STARS

Edith Head is the most celebrated costume designer in the history of US film. During her 60-year career, she worked on the costumes for approximately 1,000 films and dressed some of Hollywood's most glamorous stars, both male and female. Head was nominated 34 times for the Academy Award for best costume design, and she won eight times.[3] She was also the first woman to be the chief designer at a major film studio. Head was humble about her success, saying that "a designer is only as good as the star who wears her clothes."[4]

Retail stores hire people called clothing buyers to choose what items to sell. To see the latest styles, buyers attend fashion shows and trade shows and meet with representatives of designers and apparel manufacturers. Then buyers select what they believe consumers will buy. Once the clothing is in the store, sales associates, stock people, display artists, marketing staff, and others get to work. They make sure customers can find clothing they like. More and more stores are specializing in certain types of clothing, such as plus-size styles.

People who work in fashion advertising make sure consumers know what fashions are in style and available for sale. Their goal is to create a link between clothing designers and retail stores. The latest styles may be advertised on billboards, in magazines and newspapers, in television commercials, and in online ads.

The media also plays an important role in promoting fashion. Fashion writers and photographers attend fashion shows and report on what's new and exciting. They also observe celebrities and report what they wear—good and bad. Likewise, top-level fashion models are in great demand and may work exclusively for certain designers, advertisers, and retailers. The most successful models earn thousands of dollars an hour. However, modeling is a highly competitive business, and only a few individuals make it to this level. Most models work on a local or regional level and earn much less money. Models at all levels usually have agents who make the arrangements for their work and are paid part of the models' earnings.

A DISPLAY ARTIST

Tiffany & Co. jewelry store on Fifth Avenue in New York City has long been famous for its attention-getting window displays. And for 39 years, the person responsible for those creative displays was Gene Moore. In one typical Moore design, a bird was shown pulling a diamond necklace out of the ground as though it were a worm. Moore designed approximately 5,000 windows during his career at Tiffany. When the 88-year-old display artist died on November 23, 1998, the company paid him tribute by closing the curtains on all the store's windows for a day.[5]

FINDING YOUR PLACE IN THE FASHION INDUSTRY

How can you find your place in the fashion industry? To begin, consider whether you have an eye for style. Most of the careers in this industry—especially design careers—are based

DEFINING *STYLE*

When used to describe fashion, the word *style* is often used to mean what's currently popular. But to many people in the fashion world, true style is timeless. Someone who is stylish doesn't necessarily follow trends; rather, he or she has the confidence to wear what's flattering and attractive. French fashion designer Yves Saint Laurent captured this idea when he said, "Fashions fade. Style is eternal."[6]

on understanding and creating style.

Also consider the work skills you have. For instance, designers of all kinds must be able to sketch. Clothing designers and pattern makers, graders, and cutters need to know how clothes are constructed. And, like seamstresses and tailors, people in these careers need to be able to sew.

Having good business skills is also important. Many successful fashion designers and photographers start and build their own businesses. Doing so involves borrowing money, hiring staff, creating advertising, and deciding the prices and quantities of products. Clothing buyers also need to understand the many details involved in buying and selling merchandise.

Finally, think about your personal skills. Many careers in the fashion industry are tremendously competitive. To be successful, you must be confident and find ways of setting yourself apart from others. You also need to be able to take criticism and even failure without giving up.

In 2005, the Metropolitan Museum of Art exhibited
Chanel dresses to honor the iconic designer.

TEN POPULAR FASHION JOBS

Are you ready to explore which fashion jobs are good fits
for you? This book will cover the following jobs in depth:
clothing designer, clothing buyer, fashion photographer, and
fashion model. But first, here is a list of other popular jobs in
the field:

1. **Textile designer:** Textile designers work with
    patterns, colors, textures, and fibers to make new
    designs for fabrics. Today, some textile designers are
    developing so-called smart fabrics, which adjust to the
    environment to keep the body comfortable.

2. **Pattern maker/Grader:** A pattern maker or grader
    reproduces patterns in various sizes. Doing so allows
    people of different sizes to wear the same style.

3. **Seamstress/Tailor:** A seamstress or tailor creates,
    repairs, or alters clothing for customers.

4. **Clothing sales associate:** A clothing sales associate is
    someone who sells clothing at a store. He or she may
    help customers put together outfits.

5. **Fashion writer:** A fashion writer is someone who
    writes about fashion topics such as fashion shows,
    new collections, and advice and tips. Fashion writing
    appears in newspapers, magazines, Web sites, and
    even books.

6. **Modeling agent:** A modeling agent usually works at a modeling agency or talent agency. He or she helps models find work.

7. **Textile buyer:** A textile buyer usually works for a company that makes apparel. The buyer negotiates prices and quantities with fabric sellers to buy the fabrics the company needs.

8. **Personal shopper:** A personal shopper purchases clothing and other items for clients. The clients are individuals who are too busy to shop for themselves, unable to get to stores, or simply want help selecting clothes that are best suited for them.

9. **Display artist or designer:** This artist or designer creates displays of clothing in department stores, including window displays. He or she may also arrange merchandise in the store.

10. **Costume designer:** A costume designer creates clothing for actors to wear on stage or screen.

The fashion industry offers many opportunities for career paths. Read on to find out how you can become a part of it. Clothing designers are creating tomorrow's hot trends and clothing buyers are carefully picking out the designs they think will sell. Models are showing off new fashions. Fashion photographers are taking photos of the new styles so you can see them in fashion magazines. Fashion is everywhere.

Clothing designers display their designs at boutiques or fashion shows.

WHAT IS A CLOTHING DESIGNER?

Clothing designers create designs for just about everything people wear, from underwear to overcoats. And while the most famous designers create high-fashion clothes for the world's celebrities, most designers create everyday clothes for everyday people. Most US clothing designers specialize in creating women's wear—up to 80 percent, according to one survey.[1] The chief reason for this is that women buy more clothes than men. Women's fashions change more often than men's, and women have more variety in their clothing. Men buy fewer clothes and tend to expect what they buy to be better made and to last longer.

The greater variety in women's fashions allows for greater creativity by designers. They can even select specialties within women's wear—for example, sportswear, career, evening, bridal, and so on. Designing menswear has become more creative in recent years, however, with the addition of new styles, fabrics, and colors.

A clothing designer usually starts the creative process by sketching the item of clothing. Based on that sketch, the designer determines what pattern pieces are needed to make the garment. Next, the designer draws the pattern pieces on paper, cuts them out of an inexpensive cotton fabric, and sews them together into a rough version of the garment. After fitting the rough garment on a model and making needed changes, the designer sews a sample garment from the fabric he or she envisions for the finished piece.

The designer displays his or her collection of sample garments at showings several times a year. Clothing buyers, along with fashion writers and photographers, attend the showings to see the designer's latest fashions. High-fashion designers show their collections in exclusive runway shows, whereas less well-known designers may display their collections in their own showrooms or boutiques. In both

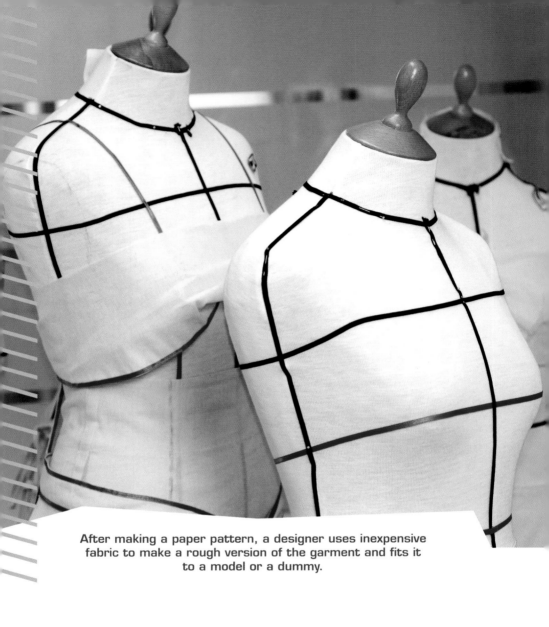

After making a paper pattern, a designer uses inexpensive fabric to make a rough version of the garment and fits it to a model or a dummy.

cases, however, the designers have the same goals: to get good reviews from the fashion media and to have buyers place orders for their clothes.

The next step is the production of the designer's fashions. For most designers, production involves the mass manufacturing of garments in many sizes and colors. Some designers stay involved in the production of their designs. Others work with a production supervisor to ensure quality and on-time delivery.

To stay ahead of production, clothing designers must work 18 to 24 months in advance.[2] For each of their two showings a year, they must create 50 to 100 new styles.[3] Like most artists, clothing designers build portfolios of their work throughout their careers—collections of sketches and photos that illustrate their range of talent and experience. Designers show their portfolios to potential customers and employers when seeking work.

HAUTE COUTURE

The world of high fashion, which is made up of the world's top designers, is sometimes referred to as *haute couture*. This French term literally means "high sewing."[4] It can be used to describe the high-fashion business, the designers in this business, or the custom-made fashions they produce.

All designers must constantly make time to learn about new styles and materials, both to stay ahead of fashion trends and to plan the next season's collection. In addition, they must seek ongoing feedback about sales from customers, salespeople, and marketing professionals. Pleasing consumers each new season is a balancing act: to ensure sales, the designer must create a unique and distinctive new look but not stray too far from the general public's taste.

Low sales or negative reviews can be disastrous for a clothing designer. Not earning the money that was expected to come in from selling a collection might mean scaling back plans for the next collection or laying off workers. And in terms of reputation, a clothing designer who has been criticized or ridiculed by the fashion media may have a hard time bouncing back.

WHAT IS A CLOTHING DESIGNER'S WORK ENVIRONMENT?

Most clothing designers work for large apparel manufacturers or design houses and create designs that fit their employers' preferences. These designers usually work in a large design studio and put in a standard eight-hour day. They tend to focus on the work of designing, leaving the work of manufacturing, marketing, and so on to employees in those departments of the company.

Self-employed designers usually have a less traditional work environment, perhaps setting up a studio at home or renting space in an office building. And because these designers are running their own businesses, they usually work longer and more irregular hours and do a wider variety of tasks. For instance, a self-employed designer might meet a client at night to show new designs, travel several hours to visit a textiles supplier, or spend the weekend sewing or fitting garments.

HOW IS THE JOB MARKET FOR CLOTHING DESIGNERS?

In 2009, US clothing designers held an estimated 15,780 jobs. Most of those jobs were located in the nation's fashion centers: New York and California. Between 2008 and 2018, an estimated 200 new jobs are expected to be created because of middle-class consumers' demand for stylish yet affordable clothing. The competition for these new jobs will be intense, especially among young designers.[5]

Designers who work for large apparel manufacturers or design houses make an average annual

DESIGNING DREAM WEDDINGS

One of the largest and most popular areas of design specialization is bridal fashion. Bridal designers create wedding gowns, along with veils, purses, gloves, shoes, and other accessories. These designers may have their own collections or create styles for bridal boutiques.

Part of the demand for original wedding fashions is that every bride wants to have her own look—one suiting both her personality and her figure. The possibilities for designing wedding gowns are almost endless due to the wide range of styles, fabrics, and decorative trims such as lace and beads.

Having a custom-made wedding gown comes at a high price. A gown specially designed by Vera Wang—the world's leading bridal designer—typically costs between $6,000 and $18,000.[6] A gown with a designer label, but not custom made, may cost between $2,000 and $4,000, and a gown at a large bridal retailer costs approximately $500.[7]

income of $61,160.[8] In general, these designers' earnings vary widely based on how many years of experience they have. Senior designers earn approximately $90,000 a year, and some earn bonuses in good sales years. Approximately one in four clothing designers is self-employed. Self-employed designers tend to have unsteady incomes, but if their work becomes popular, their chances for tremendous earnings are greater.[9]

A PROFILE OF A CLOTHING DESIGNER

Wayne Laberda always knew that he wanted a career in some kind of design. First he considered architecture, then interiors, and then graphics. But he was never really satisfied with designing until he started designing clothing. Over the years, he had been learning to sew at home and making costumes for theater productions and special events. Then one day he asked himself, "Why don't I turn a hobby I love into a career?"[10]

To achieve that goal, Laberda believes the most important thing he did was focus on his college education. At age 23, he quit his full-time job and committed himself to earning a degree in fashion design. His experience sewing and making costumes proved helpful. In his words, he had "built a solid understanding of how garments are constructed."[11] Laberda's experience with graphic design was also helpful, especially his knowledge of drawing and photo editing software.

Today, Laberda designs women's wear for a large discount retailer. The best part of his job, he says, is to see someone wearing a garment he designed: "It means they liked it enough to spend their money on it—it's pretty cool!"[12] The worst part of his job is dealing with changes in plans that come from his store's key decision makers. Laberda says, "A lot of my job is convincing them of new trends, and it can take a lot of hard work to get them to believe in something new."[13]

A DAY IN THE LIFE OF A CLOTHING DESIGNER

The most consistent task a clothing designer does on a daily basis is to keep up with communications: e-mails from customers, phone calls from manufacturers, deliveries from suppliers, and so on. Since designers work with many companies outside the United States, keeping up with communications might mean working at odd hours.

SWEATSHOPS IN THE CLOTHING INDUSTRY

Some clothing is produced in sweatshops. In these factories, people work in unhealthy and dangerous conditions. They work long hours but earn little money, and they sometimes face physical, verbal, and sexual abuse. These factories are usually located in poor countries and employ people with few options for steady work.

Producing clothes in sweatshops helps manufacturers save money and keeps down prices. However, many consumers say they would rather pay more than buy clothes made in sweatshops. Consumers can find out where designers and stores make their clothes by checking Web sites such as Responsible Shopper.

Clothing designers' work doesn't follow a day-to-day routine. Rather, it follows a cycle that includes the different stages of making a garment. To plan the next season's line, designers research fashion trends, customers' lifestyles and preferences, new sources of materials, and so on. They also sketch designs, produce patterns, sew samples, and attend fittings, or they interact with coworkers doing these tasks. Designers who work for apparel manufacturers and design houses present their designs for review and approval. They do their best to persuade their supervisors to select their work for production.

At all stages of the cycle, designers check and approve samples of fabrics, trims, colors, and so on. In some cases, checking samples may mean visiting a workshop or manufacturer, whether down the street or across the world. Senior designers may travel extensively.

The cycle comes to an exciting end during each fashion week, when designers show their new collections. Fashion weeks—held each February and November—are clothing designers' busiest times of year. Self-employed designers, in particular, may work around the clock to finish their collections and oversee all the details involved in putting on a fashion show.

A designer uses a pattern to cut out fabric in the correct size and shape for a garment.

TOP FIVE QUESTIONS ABOUT BECOMING A CLOTHING DESIGNER

1. *I already like to sketch designs for clothes. What other skills do I need to develop to become a designer?*

   You should work on developing your sewing skills. As you do, you will learn how clothes are constructed and what fabrics and trims work best for certain styles. Also work on your basic artistic skills—for instance, understanding color, texture, and other elements of design.

2. *Should I start my own business or work for an apparel manufacturer or design house?*

   Most clothing designers begin their careers at an apparel manufacturer or design house. There, they gain experience and build their portfolios. If successful, they may eventually leave and form their own businesses and clothing lines. However, remaining an employee provides more stability than forming your own business.

3. *Do I need to have a college degree to be a clothing designer?*

   No, but you will have a greater chance of success if you do. Most employers prefer to hire someone with a degree in design, communication, or business. And if you plan to be self-employed, college can help you build the skills you need to run your own business.

4. *Do I have to live in New York City to have a successful career?*

    Not necessarily, but you need to live where you can find work. In the United States, the most clothing design work is available in New York City, Los Angeles, and San Francisco.

5. *How much money will I make?*

    The average annual income of a designer who works for an apparel manufacturer or design house is $61,160.[14] Starting out, you will likely make less than this, but your salary will increase as you gain experience. If you are self-employed, your income may vary from year to year, but if your work becomes popular, you may make a lot of money.

One of the first steps to becoming a clothing designer
is learning how to sew.

WOULD YOU MAKE A GOOD CLOTHING DESIGNER?

You have always enjoyed seeing the latest fashions in magazines and on television, and you like to sketch designs of your own fashions, too. You may have even sewn clothes for yourself and your friends. Find out what other skills, education, and experience you need to turn your hobby into a career.

SKETCHING AND SEWING

Clothing design always starts with a sketch, so drawing ability is important. Other artistic skills are important, too. As a designer, you need to have an eye for detail and understand how to use color and texture effectively. You must also understand the basic principles of balance and proportion in creating pleasing designs.

Skills related to sewing are also important. Most designers are good at both hand and machine stitching. In addition, most can make and adjust patterns for their designs, because they understand how clothes are constructed. Finally, designers are familiar with different kinds of fabrics and trims and know how best to use them.

Like most jobs, clothing design has been made more efficient by the use of computers. Computer-aided design (CAD) and computer-

CAD/CAM SOFTWARE

Using CAD and CAM software, designers are able to perform many time-consuming tasks more quickly, easily, and accurately. For instance, they can create so-called virtual sample garments and view them on virtual bodies of different clothing sizes. Designers can also review color and fabric choices and adapt patterns to make different sizes of clothes. Finally, designers can create and store thousands of styles, patterns, and fabric and color combinations on the computer.

Sketching is an important skill for clothing designers.

aided manufacturing (CAM) programs, in particular, have made once-difficult tasks faster, easier, and more accurate. Designers should know how to use these forms of technology. In fact, having CAD skills is becoming increasingly important for young designers looking to get hired. Nonetheless, designers should also know how to do these tasks the old-fashioned way—by hand.

Similarly, designers should master the basic set of skills involved in clothing design, even if they plan on working for an apparel manufacturer or design house. In a large company, tasks such as pattern making and sewing are usually done by specialized workers—not designers. Even so, knowing how to do these tasks is necessary for designers to supervise coworkers and to judge others' work.

CREATIVITY, CONFIDENCE, AND COMMUNICATION

Clothing designers have a flair for pulling together colors, fabrics, and styles. They recognize trends but are also willing to head off into new directions. Having the confidence to be original is essential to success, because clothing design is a very competitive field. Designers' work is constantly reviewed—sometimes in front of coworkers and sometimes in the fashion press. Good designers must be able to learn from criticism and not take it personally.

Part of being competitive in this field is being able to work long hours and meet tight deadlines. Because making clothes is a process, delays in completing sketches or sample garments may mean lost orders and less income in the months ahead. Self-employed designers, in particular, must be willing to work long days and odd hours.

Having strong communication skills is another key to success. Designers frequently show their work to potential

DESIGNER CONFIDENCE

Ralph Lauren got his start as a designer in the late 1960s by creating a line of men's neckties.[1] When he approached retail giant Bloomingdale's, the store's buyers thought the ties were too wide. They had two requests: to make the ties narrower and to remove his name from the ties' label. Lauren refused. He was able to sell lots of ties elsewhere, however, and he built on this success to launch his own label, Polo. Bloomingdale's later bought Lauren's ties under his original terms.

customers and try to persuade them to buy. Doing so requires having good presentation and sales skills. In addition, designers are in daily contact with suppliers, manufacturers, buyers, and others. To build good work relationships, designers must communicate clearly. Understanding the teamwork involved in making clothes is also part of having productive work relationships.

CHECKLIST

Do you have what it takes to become a clothing designer? To find out, answer these questions:

- *Do you have basic artistic skills, such as the ability to sketch?*

- *Do you have basic sewing skills, such as understanding how clothes are constructed?*

- *Are you creative and original?*

- *Are you confident about your abilities?*

- *Can you learn from criticism and not take it personally?*

- *Can you work long hours and meet tight deadlines?*

- *Do you communicate clearly and persuasively?*

- *Are you able to work as part of a team?*

If you answered yes to all or most of these questions, then you have the qualities needed to be a clothing designer. If you answered no to some of the questions, figure out what you need to work on and get started. Hard work and determination can go a long way toward being successful.

HOW TO GET THERE

STARTING IN HIGH SCHOOL

In high school, choose courses that will help you develop basic artistic and sewing skills, such as drawing, design, and family and consumer sciences classes. Start a fashion notebook and practice sketching. Also practice making your own clothes. To learn more about fashion and textiles, get a job in a clothing or fabric store. To gain experience designing and sewing clothes, participate in school or local theater productions. If possible, volunteer to help at a local fashion show or beauty pageant.

DIFFERENT DEGREES

Whether you choose to start your own business or work for an apparel manufacturer or design house, your chances of success will be greater if you have a college degree. In the United States, there are approximately 200 universities, colleges, and vocational-technical schools with fashion design programs that have been endorsed by the National Association of Schools of Art and Design.[2]

Colleges and universities offer two-year associate of arts degrees and four-year bachelor degrees in fashion design, and technical schools offer certificates of design. Individuals with a two-year degree or a certificate from a vocational-technical program will probably be limited to working as a designer's assistant throughout their careers. Individuals with a four-year degree will usually begin as pattern makers or sketching assistants to a more experienced designer, but they will have opportunities for advancement.

As a student in a four-year degree program in fashion design, you will begin by taking general education courses, such as English, math, and science. In addition, you will take basic art, drawing, communications, and business classes. To be admitted into the fashion design program, you will be asked to submit your sketches and samples of your work for review. If you are admitted into the program, you will take more advanced courses in the history of design, as well as

FAMOUS SCHOOLS OF FASHION DESIGN

Two of the most famous fashion design schools in the United States are located in New York City. The Fashion Institute of Technology (FIT) was founded in 1944 for the purpose of encouraging young men and women to go into the fashion business. In 1951, FIT became part of the State University of New York and began granting associate's degrees. As of 2010, FIT granted bachelor's and master's degrees in subjects ranging from fashion design and photography to such specialties as cosmetics and fragrance marketing. That year, the school had more than 10,000 students.[3]

Parsons is the art and design school of The New School in New York. Recognizing that art and technology are linked, Parsons established programs in fashion design, interior design, and advertising and graphic design as early as 1904.[4] In 2010, Parsons offered 27 degree programs at the associate's, bachelor's, and master's levels.[5]

textiles, pattern making, tailoring, garment construction, and CAD. A student might also double major, combining a degree in fashion design with one in business, marketing, or fashion merchandising.

Many university programs arrange for their students to work as design interns or apprentices for apparel manufacturers and design houses. Being an intern or apprentice gives students an incredible opportunity not only to build valuable work experience but also to network within the fashion industry.

OPPORTUNITIES FOR ADVANCEMENT

Experienced designers can advance to any of several levels, such as chief designer, design department head, or another supervisory position. Designers at all levels work on building their portfolios. Depending on what you want to achieve in your career, you will need specific types and levels of education and experience. For instance, being the buyer for a nationwide chain of stores will require years of work at smaller stores and perhaps a regional chain.

Clothing buyers decide which clothes
stores will offer each season.

WHAT IS A
CLOTHING BUYER?

Clothing buyers work on the business side of
fashion. Working for a boutique, department store,
or chain of stores, they purchase clothing from designers,
manufacturers, and wholesalers for sale in the store or

stores. Deciding what to buy requires knowing the tastes and needs of both the store and its customers. Making bad decisions can be disastrous.

High-fashion buyers, who work for exclusive stores and boutiques, see fashion designers' new collections twice a year. During fashion weeks, these buyers travel to New York City, Paris, and Milan to visit designers' showrooms and to attend their fashion shows. Then, the buyers select the clothes they believe their customers will buy.

Buyers for department stores and chain stores also attend fashion shows and trade shows, where they meet with the representatives of clothing designers and manufacturers. These buyers travel to secondary fashion centers—such as Dallas, Atlanta, and Chicago—during market weeks, which are held four to six times a year. Like high-fashion buyers, these buyers must choose the clothes they think will sell well in their stores.

Because of the time needed to design, sew, and manufacture clothing, clothing buyers work at least one season ahead of when the clothes will be in the store. For instance, a buyer may select fall and winter clothing in the spring. In some cases, buyers work two or three seasons ahead. The clothing they select arrives in stores six or more months later.

Before buying anything, a clothing buyer must have a plan. That plan is based on a budget set by the retail store or its headquarters. The budget tells the buyer how much he or she can spend for a given fashion season. The buyer is responsible not only for staying within that budget but also

THE OUTLOOK FOR ONLINE RETAIL

A report by Forrester Research, a company that does marketing research, predicted that much of the growth of US retail after 2010 would come from Internet sales. In fact, by 2014, online retail sales were expected to reach $249 billion. Consumers will make approximately one in 12 purchases online, according to the report.[1]

Interestingly, the downturn in the US economy is believed to be one of the reasons that consumers are going online. Crosschecking prices from one retailer to another is easier on computer than on foot. Likewise, doing research into product features and availabilities is fast and easy online. Also, most merchandise can be ordered online and shipped, saving consumers a trip to the store. And in some cases, shipping is even free.

Online retail is especially strong for clothes, shoes, and accessories. Yet some consumers still want to make their purchases at a store. Some might look around online but actually buy at the store. According to the Forrester study, this might be explained by differences in customer service between stores and online retailers.

for getting the most merchandise possible for the money.

The clothing buyer's plan is also based on a variety of information about the store and its customers. For instance, the buyer must understand the store's reputation, goals, and sales history. The buyer must also understand the store's customers. Hearing the opinions of loyal customers is a good way to find out whether previous buying decisions have been on target.

Finally, the buyer's plan must take into account developments in the fashion industry. This includes trends in style as well as consumer behavior. Buyers can get this information by attending fashion shows, examining industry reports, and reading trade publications. Buyers can also stay in touch with their local market by visiting area stores and observing shoppers at malls.

WHAT IS A CLOTHING BUYER'S WORK ENVIRONMENT?

Buying clothes for a living might sound like a fun job, but being a clothing buyer is tough work. Buyers often work long and irregular hours, including many evenings and weekends. They work especially long hours when retail is at its busiest, such as in the fall, which is back-to-school time, and around the Christmas holidays. During these times, buyers may spend most of the day on the store's sales floor, checking merchandise, advising sales associates and display artists, and observing and talking to customers.

Clothing buyers are busiest of all just before and after fashion weeks and market weeks. Before these weeks, buyers review sales and inventory data and plan which suppliers they will see and perhaps buy from. After these weeks, buyers complete order forms and issue contracts to the suppliers they are buying from. During these times, buyers spend long hours attending meetings with marketing staff and doing paperwork in their offices.

Like people in other fashion careers, buyers sometimes have to relocate to find work. The most buying jobs are in New York City and Los Angeles. Others are available in secondary US fashion markets and other large cities.

HOW IS THE JOB MARKET FOR CLOTHING BUYERS?

In 2009, approximately 2,120 Americans were employed as buyers in clothing stores.[2] Some sources believe the number of jobs in this field will grow because of the huge number and variety of products available for sale worldwide, both in stores and on the Internet. Others believe that mergers and acquisitions among clothing stores will result in lost jobs.

In May 2009, the annual median income of a clothing buyer was $45,850.[3] A buyer's potential for earnings depends on the kind of store he or she works for. Large department stores and chain stores, which have huge volumes of sales, tend to pay the highest salaries. Some buyers are also paid bonuses when the store has a good sales year. In addition, buyers usually receive a discount when they shop where they work.

THE NEED FOR BUYERS

In the past, individual stores were usually locally owned and served only local customers. The owners of these stores did the buying and the marketing of merchandise. This practice changed during the twentieth century with the growth of large department stores and retail chains. Running these stores was complicated and required many kinds of specialized workers—including buyers. Buyers were also needed because of the greater variety of merchandise that became available. Viewing, ordering, and scheduling the delivery of merchandise became a demanding job.

Do you anticipate fashion trends? If so, you might make a good clothing buyer!

A PROFILE OF A CLOTHING BUYER

Maggie Mullen is a buyer for a retail Web site that sells women's sleepwear. She got her job through a clothing supplier she worked with at an earlier job. Making connections is one of the keys to developing a career as a buyer, Mullen believes. She says, "Every person you meet could influence your next job, . . . so cherish each conversation and relationship."[4]

CERTIFICATION OF BUYERS

Clothing buyers aren't currently required to be certified, but they may be in the future. Individuals in other purchasing professions must be certified by an organization such as the American Purchasing Society or the National Association of Purchasing Management. The purpose of certification is to ensure that people involved in high levels of purchasing have the necessary skills and knowledge. For most certifications, the individual must have a specific level of work experience, meet education requirements, and pass both written and oral tests.

Mullen also believes in the importance of getting on-the-job experience early. She worked in several types of retail stores during high school and college, including a clothing store, a department store, and a coffee and gift shop. Having this early work experience, according to Mullen, "really helped to increase my understanding of how a store operates."[5] Volunteer work, she notes, can provide valuable opportunities as well. While working on her bachelor's degree in merchandise management, Mullen joined a volunteer student organization that allowed her to work on window displays and help with fashion shows.

Mullen has been a buyer for seven years. She enjoys the balance of creative and analytical skills involved in her work. She also likes traveling to attend trade shows and to meet with product representatives. Mullen admits that working long hours to reach deadlines is tough. Working under deadlines "can lead to stressful days," she says.[6]

A DAY IN THE LIFE OF A CLOTHING BUYER

A clothing buyer usually starts the day in his or her office, looking over records of the previous day's sales. Buyers are constantly analyzing sales data to see whether the store is meeting its financial goals. In addition, buyers are always trying to come up with strategies for improving sales. Early in the day, the buyer may also check with the store's warehouse to see whether shipments have arrived. He or she may cancel an order that's running late and think about ordering a replacement item instead.

About half of a clothing buyer's day is spent in meetings. For example, a buyer may meet with the store's marketing group to review plans for distributing merchandise among the store's different locations. A buyer might also meet with sales managers and associates to provide training and answer questions about the store's merchandise. A planner usually helps a buyer distribute product to stores. A buyer will also train and advise sales associates and display artists while spending time on the sales floor. Buyers are so involved in the general operation of the store that they need to be part of many discussions and decisions.

On some days, a clothing buyer will visit the showroom of a local supplier to see the newest merchandise. After seeing the fashions, the buyer discusses details of price, quantity, and schedule with the supplier's representative. By late afternoon, the buyer has usually decided what to buy. During these daylong visits, buyers enjoy being offered a wide

Buyers attend fashion shows to decide which styles their stores should feature in upcoming seasons.

assortment of foods and beverages. Suppliers do their best to make buyers feel relaxed and comfortable, hoping their hospitality will result in good sales.

Throughout the day, the buyer checks e-mail and voice mail to respond to questions from supervisors and suppliers. He or she spends a lot of time on the computer tending to paperwork, such as filling out order forms and issuing purchase orders. Buyers also go online to do ongoing research into trends, new product lines, marketing strategies, and other topics.

TOP FIVE QUESTIONS ABOUT BECOMING A CLOTHING BUYER

1. *I'm always on top of the latest fashion trends. Would I make a good clothing buyer?*

   Following fashion trends is certainly one of the important things buyers do. Keep in mind, though, that buyers work one or more seasons ahead of when fashions are in stores. So, knowing what's in style now isn't especially helpful in deciding what fashions to buy for a year from now. In addition to knowing about fashion trends, buyers need to know about trends in consumer behavior.

2. *What kinds of jobs should I do in high school to prepare for a career as a buyer?*

   Work in retail to learn how stores operate. Working in a small clothing store would be ideal, because you would get the most hands-on experience with the different kinds of jobs that are done at a store— including buying, perhaps.

3. *Do I need to have a college degree to be a clothing buyer?*

   No, but having a college degree will help you get your first job and improve your chances for advancement later in your career. Most clothing buyers have a bachelor's degree in fashion merchandising, marketing, advertising, or general business. Some buyers have also studied fashion design or textiles.

4. *I really want to buy fashions for my favorite department store. How can I get a job there?*
   Early in your career, you won't likely get a job as a buyer in a department store. Rather, you will start working at the store as a sales associate or buyer's assistant and work your way up. Many buyers start out working for a small store or boutique and then move to a department store or chain of stores.

5. *Where should I look for a job as a clothing buyer?*
   In the United States, the majority of buying jobs are available in New York City and Los Angeles. Others are available in secondary US fashion markets, such as Chicago, Atlanta, and Dallas. Although most large cities have department stores, buying for those stores is probably done on a regional or national basis, not locally.

Students who want to be buyers can gain experience
as sales associates.

WOULD YOU MAKE A GOOD CLOTHING BUYER?

You love to follow fashion trends and see what new clothes are in stores at the start of each season. You also notice what clothes are left on the "clearance" rack at the end of each season—and you think you know why! Paying attention to styles and sales is something clothing buyers do on a daily basis. Find out what other skills, education, and experience you need to have a career as a clothing buyer.

UNDERSTANDING CLOTHES AND CUSTOMERS

Having an eye for fashion is certainly necessary for being a buyer. Clothing buyers must know about clothes and fabrics, including details of style, fit, size, color, care, and cost. Buyers must also be able to forecast trends in fashion and customer spending a year or more in advance. Choosing the right merchandise means understanding customers' tastes and buying behaviors.

Some buyers, especially those in smaller stores, get involved in fashion

KEEPING CUSTOMERS HAPPY

A study conducted in 2007 called "The Department Store Experience" looked at reasons customers shop at department stores. It found that customers decide where to shop based mostly on "appealing fashions and styles of merchandise." However, customers' overall shopping experience was affected most by the quality of service provided by the sales staff.

Among upscale department stores, Neiman Marcus and Nordstrom were rated the highest in overall customer satisfaction. Customers at these stores were mostly interested in exclusive merchandise and good customer service. Among midscale department stores, JCPenney, Kohl's, and Macy's were rated the highest. Customers at these stores were mostly concerned with price and value.[1]

merchandising. Merchandising involves deciding how to price, display, advertise, and sell clothing in the store. By analyzing sales and inventory, buyers keep track of what is and isn't selling. Buyers must also have the business skills needed to understand retail.

MAKING GOOD DECISIONS

Having good decision-making skills is another key part of being a successful clothing buyer. Good buyers are able to review all their options and determine the best course to follow—sometimes working with tight budgets and strict deadlines. Buyers are also able to prioritize goals to do what's best for their employer.

Clothing buyers must also use good judgment in deciding which suppliers to buy from. Buyers must evaluate, for example, whether a supplier seems likely to deliver merchandise on time. When there's a problem with an order, buyers must be direct and clear about what needs to be done.

In addition to suppliers, buyers interact with a wide range of people at the stores where they work. Leadership skills are helpful when training and advising sales associates, display artists, and others. Buyers also need the confidence and polish to interact with their supervisors and maybe even the store's president or owner. Most buyers are outgoing and show their enthusiasm for their work.

Being well organized is also essential. Buyers keep track of many different kinds of information in their work, ordering merchandise, monitoring inventory, tracking prices and

Clothing buyers need to be familiar
with customers' shopping habits.

markdowns, and managing schedules. Being well organized
is also important because buyers work several months in
advance of when merchandise is actually sold.

In the end, buyers must make decisions that will be
profitable for their stores. Making good decisions will result

in strong sales, happy customers, and high earnings. Making bad decisions will result in unsold merchandise, frustrated customers, and lost money. Making too many bad decisions— say, several seasons in a row—will damage the reputation of the store and drive away customers. It may also cost the buyer his or her job. Knowing this, buyers must be able to face criticism and failure without losing confidence.

CHECKLIST

Do you have what it takes to become a clothing buyer? To find out, answer these questions:

- *Do you follow trends and have an eye for fashion?*

- *Do you have a basic understanding of retail?*

- *Are you good at tracking information?*

- *Can you consider several choices and goals and then make a good decision?*

- *Do you communicate clearly with others—even being direct when there's a problem?*

- *Do you have good leadership skills?*

- *Do you have strong analytical or math skills?*

- *Can you accept criticism and setbacks without losing confidence?*

If you answered yes to all or most of these questions, then you have the qualities needed to be a buyer. If you answered no to some of the questions, work on developing those qualities.

HOW TO GET THERE

WORKING IN HIGH SCHOOL

You can start preparing for a career as a clothing buyer while still in high school. Take courses in fashion design and merchandising, if they are offered, along with business, math, and economics courses. To learn more about retailing, work part time in a clothing store—maybe over the summer or the busy holiday season. Working in a small store, especially, will help you learn about buying and marketing clothes.

GOING TO COLLEGE

There are several schools that focus on fashion careers, such as LIM College

BUILDING A CAREER

Large department stores and chain stores often provide in-house training programs for employees who want to advance into positions as buyers or executives. These programs are usually open only to college graduates. Most of these programs last four months. During that time, trainees usually work in a variety of departments within the store, gaining experience in all areas of operation. Classroom sessions taught by senior buyers and executives are part of the program as well. After completing the program, trainees are put in junior management positions for additional supervision and training.

and Fashion Institute of Design and Merchandising (FIDM). Most clothing buyers have a bachelor's degree in fashion merchandising, marketing, advertising, or general business. But, whatever major you select for your college degree, you should take courses in accounting, economics, finance, advertising, and marketing. You should also take business courses that focus on communication, management, and computer applications.

To deepen your knowledge of fashion, you might get a minor in fashion design or textiles. Some students combine a degree in fashion merchandising with one in marketing or management. University programs often help students get internships in fashion merchandising. Being an intern will give you the opportunity to get valuable work experience and to network with professionals in the fashion industry.

MANY EMPLOYMENT OPTIONS

Clothing buyers have many options for employment in both retail and wholesale. They may work for small stores and boutiques, department stores, or national and international chains of stores.

Most buyers start out as sales associates or buyers' assistants and work their way up. Many begin by working for a small store or boutique and then move to a department store or chain of stores. A sales associate in a department store or chain store may eventually be promoted to a position called head of stock. This position involves tracking inventory and keeping the merchandise in order. The head of stock may supervise several employees. He or she also passes on communication between the sales associates and the buyer.

The next promotion may be to the position of assistant buyer or assistant merchandiser. Both of these positions involve more hands-on work with buying, pricing, and marketing. Someone at the assistant level will also support the buyer by conducting research, helping process orders, following schedules, and whatever else needs doing. And with success in this position, the assistant will eventually become a buyer.

MANAGEMENT POSITIONS

Successful buyers are sometimes promoted to management positions in the store. The merchandise manager, for example, supervises other buyers, helps set policies about quantities and prices of items, and coordinates buying and selling among different

STORES' NATIONAL HEADQUARTERS

Although most large cities have department stores, the buying for those stores is probably done on a regional or national basis. Becoming a buyer for a department store may mean moving to one of these cities:

- Bloomingdale's—New York, New York
- JCPenney—Plano, Texas, near Dallas
- Kohl's—Menomonee Falls, Wisconsin, near Milwaukee
- Macy's—Cincinnati, Ohio, and New York, New York
- Neiman Marcus—Dallas, Texas
- Nordstrom—Seattle, Washington
- Sears—Hoffman Estates, Illinois, near Chicago

departments. Eventually, the merchandise manager might supervise several regional divisions of a store or become an upper-level executive, such as vice president of purchasing or merchandising. Because buyers are involved with the entire operation of a store, they are well qualified to move into top-level leadership positions.

Some buyers are involved with fashion merchandising, which includes pricing, displaying, and advertising clothing.

Successful fashion photographers develop a style that sets them apart.

WHAT IS A FASHION PHOTOGRAPHER?

Fashion photographers may work in any of several areas of the fashion business. Most work in the advertising industry, shooting the photos used to sell clothes. Their work might appear in ads in newspapers and magazines, on billboards and Web sites, or on signs in malls and stores. Other photographers shoot the artwork that accompanies articles in fashion magazines and trade publications. Still other photographers do catalog work, shooting photos that will appear in the print and online versions of catalogs.

Some fashion photographers are employees of advertising agencies, fashion magazines, design houses, retail stores, and photography studios. But more than half of all fashion photographers work freelance, which means they are self-employed.[1] Some freelance photographers are under contract with an advertising agency, magazine publisher, or other business. Having a contract means the photographer will get work from this business on a regular basis and for a set fee. Other freelance photographers operate their own studios and may have their own employees. These photographers usually work for many different businesses and for a range of fees and terms.

At a photo shoot, the fashion photographer takes

PHOTO STYLISTS

Many photographers insist that having a successful photo shoot depends, in large part, on having a good photo stylist. The photo stylist works with the art or creative director and the photographer to plan the desired image or mood for the photography. Then, the stylist works on creating that image or mood, finding the right props, backgrounds, accessories, and even locations. The stylist may also hire the models and makeup artists for the shoot. In addition to being creative, a good stylist must be organized, resourceful, flexible, and patient.

direction from an art director or creative director. The director has in mind a specific mood or theme that the photographer is intended to capture. The photographer also works with a photo stylist, who sets up the different shots, and hair stylists and makeup artists, who prepare the models. In order to get the kinds of shots he or she wants, the photographer directs the models.

Like other artists, photographers must create a portfolio, or a collection of work. A good portfolio shows a range and variety of photographs from across one's career. The photographer shows his or her portfolio to new clients in the hope of getting work. Some freelance photographers also have agents who help get them work.

WHAT IS A FASHION PHOTOGRAPHER'S WORK ENVIRONMENT?

Oddly enough, being a photographer can be isolating, even lonely. Most photographers spend only a small part of the day taking photos. Much of their time is spent alone at the computer, working with digital images. They may work in a studio or from home.

A photo shoot may be done in a photography studio or on location at some carefully selected place—maybe inside the lobby of a famous hotel or outdoors at a baseball field. Most photographers prefer to shoot in a studio, because they have better control of lighting and other conditions than when working on location.

Fashion photographers sometimes travel to do photo shoots outdoors or on location.

Fashion photography is a very competitive field. To become successful, fashion photographers must develop a style or technique that sets them apart. They must also be able to work long and sometimes odd hours. Shooting fashion involves working at a hectic pace and meeting tight deadlines.

Another difficulty photographers may face is working with demanding personalities. Many different people are involved in a photo shoot, and they may not always agree on how things should be done. Also, plans may change at the last minute, and people may be late or not show up at all. Through it all, the photographer must be patient and professional.

HOW IS THE JOB MARKET FOR FASHION PHOTOGRAPHERS?

In 2008, photographers of all kinds (not just fashion) held approximately 152,000 jobs in the United States. More than half of them were self-employed, which is higher than in most professions. Among photographers who were employees, the average income was $29,440.[2]

Self-employed, or freelance, photographers tend to earn less than salaried photographers. Freelance photographers are usually paid by the job. Their fee usually depends on their experience and reputation. A beginning photographer may earn $250 for a job, while an established photographer may earn $2,500. A photographer with a national reputation may earn $100,000 or more a year.[3]

The outlook for work in fashion photography is mixed. Some companies have laid off their salaried photographers and hired freelancers. While this means that more freelance work is available, it also means there are more freelancers competing for jobs. Developments in digital technology have

A PERSONAL STYLE

Chad Boutin has been a freelance photographer for 20 years, including 12 years shooting fashion. His clients have included Redken and Avon, and his work has appeared in *Vogue*. Boutin offers this advice for getting started as a photographer: "Get your name attached to a style. Clients compensate me for a style, not because I own a camera. My camera plays a minor role in what I do. I direct. I put my style in a scene."[4]

also eliminated work for photographers. Because of the reduced cost and greater ease of using a digital camera, some individuals now take their own photos rather than hire a photographer. Also, the use of computer software to change digital photos means that existing photos can be altered again and again, rather than reshot.

A PROFILE OF A FASHION PHOTOGRAPHER

Ramon Moreno has been a fashion photographer for 15 years. After going to a photography school in Florida, he worked as an assistant for several photographers. Then one day, he thought, "I can do this on my own!" Looking back, he explained, "I just made up my mind that this is what I wanted to do, and I went for it."[5]

Moreno believes in the importance of knowing one's craft—of being "better at it than anyone else."[6] He has made good use of available sources in developing his own skills. For instance, he has studied fashion magazines and the work of other photographers. He has also taken video lessons offered online about photography subjects such as using light. Like most photographers, Moreno is passionate about the importance of light in photography. He recommends, "Study lighting every day. Every moment, it's all around us. It has so many characteristics, from sunny to moody."[7] As the owner and operator of Ramon Moreno Photography, Moreno also knows the importance of having good business skills— marketing skills, in particular. He offers this advice to others interested in being a fashion photographer: "Follow your vision. Do not take no for an answer. So many people are negative. You need to keep going for what you want."[8]

A DAY IN THE LIFE OF A FASHION PHOTOGRAPHER

Much of a fashion photographer's day is spent talking on the phone and managing e-mail. Scheduling client meetings and photo shoots often means juggling many people's schedules. To make arrangements for a photo shoot, the photographer may have to line up transportation, visit locations, and put together a team of stylists.

To prepare for a photo shoot, the photographer must arrive early and set up the studio or location. That involves assembling the sets, positioning the lighting, and setting up the computer. The photographer also has to do a lighting test to check for quality and consistency. When shooting outdoors, changes in lighting, weather, and other conditions might mean having to make continual adjustments. Changing conditions might mean delays in shooting as well.

Most days, fashion photographers spend a lot of time doing postproduction. For example, they download images from the camera to the computer, make color corrections, touch up the images, and so on. In this age of digital photography, few photographers shoot and develop film.

Photographers often work in studios so they can control the lighting.

TOP FIVE QUESTIONS ABOUT BECOMING A FASHION PHOTOGRAPHER

1. *What can I do now to prepare myself for a career as a fashion photographer?*

   Work on developing your basic photography skills. Get a good camera and carry it with you as much as possible. Take photography classes at your school, at a local camera store, or through a community education program. Also take computer classes to learn how to use graphics software. Getting a job at a camera store or a photography studio could help you learn about equipment and techniques. Also look at fashion magazines and go to photography exhibits.

2. *How can I get photography work?*

   Begin by shooting photos for free to get experience and start your portfolio. You may be able to publish photos in your school's yearbook or newspaper. Try your local newspaper, too. Look for photo contests that you can enter. Once you have some experience, look for work as a photographer's assistant.

3. *How much does it cost to get started?*

   You can buy a good digital camera for between $500 and $1,000—less if you shop for used equipment.[9] The estimated cost of starting a freelance photography business ranges from $3,000 to $12,000.[10]

4. *How do I know if I'm good enough to be a fashion photographer?*

   Ask yourself these questions instead: Do I take interesting photographs? Do my family, friends, and teachers compliment me on my photographs or ask me to bring my camera to events with them? If so, then you likely have the skills. But remember, you may still have a long way to go!

5. *How much money will I make?*

   In 2009, salaried photographers earned an average of $29,770 per year.[11] However, the pay scale for photographers is dependent on where they live, who they photograph, and whether they are freelancers.

Learning how to use a camera now is the first step to a career in photography.

WOULD YOU MAKE A GOOD FASHION PHOTOGRAPHER?

You often carry a camera with you, and you have taken some amazing photos. You have an eye for detail, seeing things that other people just don't see. You are also interested in fashion as an art form—not just as models wearing clothes. Find out what other skills, education, and experience you need to have a career as a fashion photographer.

VISUALIZING A SCENE

Having an eye for detail is an essential skill for a fashion photographer. But just as important is being able to visualize a scene or design. Unlike many kinds of photographers who wait for a scene to occur, fashion photographers mostly create their own scenes.

To be able to visualize a scene, fashion photographers must have a good understanding of light. They must also understand basic principles of composition in art, including color, texture, balance, and proportion. Finally, photographers must have good eyesight and good hand-eye coordination.

KEEP GOOD NOTES

Experienced photographers recommend keeping a journal in which you make notes about the different photos you take. For each photo, write down the shutter speed, aperture, and other camera settings you used, plus other details about light, distance, and so on. Then review your notes against the actual photos. Figure out how you created the shots you like and don't like. Then shoot more photos applying what you learned.

Successful fashion photographers are highly creative and imaginative. They are also willing to take risks in their work. Most well-known photographers have a unique style or technique that sets their work apart.

TECHNOLOGY SAVVY

Being a fashion photographer also requires a lot of technical skill. Photographers must know how to use different cameras, lenses, and filters to work in certain conditions and to achieve certain effects. Photographers should also have experience in both color and black-and-white photography. In the twenty-first century, technology has revolutionized the photography business. In taking digital photos, most photographers still prefer to operate the camera manually rather than use its automatic settings. Understanding the new technologies is critical to a career as a fashion photographer.

BEING COOPERATIVE AND CLEAR

As part of the team that works at a fashion shoot, fashion photographers must be cooperative. When faced with delays, changes, and other problems, they must be patient and flexible. Taking a creative approach to problem solving has resulted in some photographers doing amazing work.

Fashion photographers often give and get directions, so they must be clear and detailed in communicating with others. And when communicating with models, in particular, fashion photographers must help them feel relaxed and confident. Photographers must also be relaxed and confident to get the shots they need for the client.

RUNNING A STUDIO

For a freelance fashion photographer, one of the biggest responsibilities is setting up a studio. That involves renting or buying studio space and purchasing and maintaining the necessary equipment. Because of ongoing advances in technology, new equipment is often needed.

Self-employed photographers must also set fees, bill clients, and collect payments for their work. When starting out, especially, photographers may be expected to cover their own expenses. More experienced photographers may be allowed to bill the client for their expenses, which requires keeping records.

Freelance fashion photographers must also understand the legal issues involved in their work. They need to know how to write contracts that identify the terms under which their work can be used. Writing contracts and negotiating with clients requires an understanding of licensing and copyright laws.

GETTING CREDIT

When a photographer's work is published, it usually carries a byline that identifies him or her as the photographer. Photographers who are just starting out should insist on getting a byline when their work is published, even in a small publication such as a school newspaper. New photographers should be cautious of publications that don't want to provide credit or that want to use a photo on an unlimited basis without payment or other compensation. Be aware that the terms of some photo contests state that the winner gives up all rights to his or her photo.

Perhaps the biggest challenge in being self-employed is getting work. Freelance photographers are constantly marketing their businesses. Most photographers display their portfolios online, which makes their Web sites their primary marketing tools.

CHECKLIST

Do you have what it takes to become a fashion photographer? To find out, answer these questions:

- *Do you have an eye for detail and the ability to visualize scenes?*

- *Do you see the artistry in fashion?*

- *Do you have basic photographic knowledge and skills? If not, are you willing to learn them?*

- *Are you cooperative, flexible, and patient in working with others?*

- *Are you clear and detailed in communicating with others?*

- *Can you remain relaxed and confident even in a hectic situation?*

- *Are you interested in running your own business?*

If you answered yes to all or most of these questions, then you have the qualities needed to be a photographer. If you answered no to some of the questions, you might need to work on your skills. Still, don't give up on your dream. With

*some determination and willingness to learn, you may make
it as a fashion photographer.*

HOW TO GET THERE

GAIN EXPERIENCE

To prepare for being a fashion photographer, work on
developing your general photography skills. Take photography
classes. Also take computer classes to learn how to use
graphics software. If you can, get a job in a camera store or a
photography studio.

In addition, work on developing your artistic skills. Take
studio arts classes in various media, such as painting and
drawing. Also look at magazines that are well known for their
photography, such as *Vogue* and *National Geographic*. Attend
exhibits that feature the work of well-known photographers.
Finally, carry your camera with you often, and look for
opportunities to take interesting photos.

To start building your portfolio, take photos for your
school newspaper or yearbook. Also take photos of local
events and send them to your local newspaper. Look into
photo contests, which are sometimes sponsored by camera
stores. When submitting your work, always ask for a byline,
a credit that identifies you as the photographer. Be careful
about protecting your rights to your work. In particular, don't
allow anyone to use your work multiple times or in multiple
places without getting your permission in writing.

Beyond high school, you should continue your education
and training to develop strong technical skills. You can

Fashion photographers' work can appear in magazines, in catalogs, on billboards, or in other advertisements.

acquire those skills by completing a photography program at a trade school or vocational-technical school. You can also enroll in a college or university and take fashion photography courses as part of a two-year or four-year degree program in photojournalism or commercial art. Many of these programs include courses in business and marketing, which will be helpful if you decide to work freelance.

GOING TO WORK

Many fashion photographers start out as photographers' assistants or trainees. Although doing these jobs may involve a lot of moving lights and hauling equipment, assistants or trainees are expected to have basic photography skills. Working in one of these positions offers a new photographer a good chance to observe a professional at work and to develop the artistic, photographic, and business skills needed to be successful. Attending photo shoots, fashion shows, and other events also provides a great chance to network.

After gaining some experience as an assistant or trainee, a fashion photographer may decide to work on his or her own. Starting one's own business is expensive, though. The necessary equipment can cost up to $12,000.[1] Additional money will be needed for studio space, supplies, and possibly staff. To earn enough money to support themselves, many new fashion photographers do other kinds of work, such as portraits and weddings.

Advancement in this field comes with positive recognition.

PROFESSIONAL PHOTOGRAPHERS OF AMERICA

The Professional Photographers of America (PPA) is the largest nonprofit organization of professional photographers in the world. It has more than 22,000 members in 54 countries. The goals of the PPA are expressed in the group's mission statement: "to be the leader in the dissemination of knowledge in the areas of professional business practices and creative image-making, and to define and maintain the industry's standards of excellence." Membership in the PPA costs $194 a year for aspiring professional photographers and $323 a year for active professionals. One of the many benefits of membership is receiving the monthly journal *Professional Photographer*.[2]

Successful photographers are known for work that's creative and unique. They are also known for doing high-quality photography that's on schedule and on budget. Even so, it can take years of hard work to build a successful photography business.

Salaried photographers who work for advertising agencies, fashion magazines, and so on may advance within their companies. For instance, they may be promoted to a senior or supervisory photographer position, or they may become an art director or creative director. Senior-level photographers may also be assigned to specific accounts or clients. Many salaried fashion photographers leave their jobs and start their own studios.

A beginning photographer should always
have a camera nearby.

8

Runway models are very busy during fashion week in New York City.

WHAT IS A FASHION MODEL?

Quite simply, fashion models are hired to wear clothes to make consumers want to buy them. Seeing a pair of jeans, for instance, on a fit, attractive, stylish young woman will make many other women want to own that same pair of jeans. Models not only make the clothes look good, but they also make people feel good about owning and wearing the clothes.

Some fashion models make live appearances. So-called runway models wear the latest designs in fashion shows that are attended by fashion buyers, writers, and photographers. Live models may also show fashions to consumers at local department stores, boutiques, and malls. Models prepare for these shows by attending fittings and rehearsals.

Most models display fashions in printed publications,

TAKING YOUR OWN PHOTOS

If you want to submit your own photos to a modeling or talent agency rather than having professional photos taken, you should ask a friend or family member to take these shots of you:

1. Two head shots facing straight forward—one smiling and one not—with your hair down.

2. A head shot facing straight forward—smiling—with your hair pulled, clipped, or gelled up and off your face. This shot is intended to show your facial features as well as your ears, jaw, and neck.

3. A profile head shot with your hair off your face. This shot is to show the side angles of your neck and jawbone.

4. A neutral clothed three-quarters shot of your body, from your lower hips to the top of your head. To make the shot more interesting, turn your shoulders slightly if you are a woman and hook your thumb in your pants pocket if you are a man. Think in terms of shaping your upper body, rather than posing.

5. Two full-length shots of your body: one from the front and one from the back.

such as catalogs, magazines, and newspapers. These models are photographed at photo shoots. To prepare for a shoot, models work with makeup artists and hair stylists.

Most models get work through a modeling or talent agency. Acting as the model's representative, the agency sets up jobs in fashion shows, photo shoots, and more. The agency trains the model to develop a certain image—perhaps exotic or wholesome. The agency then promotes the model to clients looking for someone with that image.

Models are also expected to promote themselves. All models—and especially new models—must have test photographs taken. Testing, as it's called, provides new material for the model's portfolio, or book. A model's book is a collection of photos showing his or her range of work. Because styles change constantly, models must test on a regular basis to update their portfolios.

Models bring their books with them when they meet with potential clients. Agencies usually arrange these meetings, which are sometimes called "go-sees." Specifically, agencies send models to castings, which are auditions or interviews where the client is seeking a certain kind of model, and open calls, which are more general requests. The job or assignment a model receives is called a booking.

WHAT IS A FASHION MODEL'S WORK ENVIRONMENT?

Being a fashion model can be glamorous and exciting, but it can also mean working long, hard hours. For example, doing a fashion show might involve hours of fittings, rehearsals, and styling of hair and makeup. And doing a photo shoot might involve traveling to an out-of-the-way location and spending hours posing in extreme weather conditions. No matter what the circumstances, the model must be flexible and cooperative.

Another difficult part of being a fashion model is the high level of competition. One hundred models may show up for the same casting, but only one of them will get the job. Because of the competitive nature of this work, models must get used to hearing criticisms of their appearance.

FACING THE CRITICS

Former model Judy Goss offers new models this advice: "I don't care what you look like, or who you think you are or can be, someone is going to turn you down for something, and most likely it will happen again and again, because success in the modeling industry is not based on any objective criteria. . . . Since everyone is going to tell you different things about your looks, let their comments fly over your head if they are not saying what you want to hear."[2]

HOW IS THE JOB MARKET FOR FASHION MODELS?

In 2008, models held about 2,200 jobs in the United States, and that number is expected to grow to about 2,500 by 2018.[1] More work is expected to be available because of the increased advertising of products and the use of new media, such as the Internet.

Most models are paid by the hour. In small fashion markets, models are paid $75 to $150 an hour, and in larger markets, they are paid $200 to $500 an hour.[3] The agency that represents a model usually takes 10 to 20 percent of his or her earnings.[4]

A model who works steadily in a local market can make $100,000 a year, but most models earn far less than that.[5] In 2008, the average US model made about $27,000, or an average of $13 an hour.[6] As noted earlier, the competition for modeling jobs is tough. Also, few models work every day, and many modeling jobs involve only a few hours' work. Most models must also have a part-time job to support themselves.

Some models find work by specializing. Plus-size models, elderly models, and ethnic models are in more demand than ever before. Americans today want to see more diversity and models that look more like them. Some models also specialize in body parts, such as hands, feet, legs, and even teeth.

A PROFILE OF A FASHION MODEL

Tearra Rosario didn't start out wanting to be a fashion model. She began modeling part time while going to college. A few years after graduating, she decided to pursue "creative projects": modeling, acting and being a singer, songwriter, and drummer.[7] She explained, "I didn't realize that my primary job had turned into modeling until I started putting my résumé together and looked at the work I was doing. Time flies when you're doing what you love, and I was having a blast."[8]

Rosario believes that the acting, dancing, and singing programs she participated in while growing up developed the focus needed to be a model. In addition, taking part in these programs helped her become comfortable with her body and with expressing herself through her appearance and movements. That didn't come naturally to her. As a child, she was quite shy and found it hard to communicate effectively with others.

After some early success as a runway model, Rosario became "completely driven to find more work."[9] She eventually signed on with three agencies to find work in all her arts. What she likes most about being a model is "having the opportunity to inspire and be inspired by creatively talented people."[10] She also loves being transformed into another person by changing her appearance. "It's like dressing up for Halloween every time I go to work," she says.[11] The hardest

MEN AT WORK

Modeling is one of the few careers in which women are usually paid more than men. That was confirmed in a 2009 interview with Russian model Matvey Lykov, who's considered one of the top 25 male models in the world. In one year, after walking the runway in 34 high-fashion shows, he earned an estimated $40,000 before taxes. For 11 of the shows, he was paid in clothing, not cash.[12]

Despite having lower earnings, men tend to have longer careers than women. The reason seems to be that society is more accepting of aging men than aging women. This attitude is changing somewhat, though, as more elderly models both male and female are being hired.

Models get ready for photo shoots by working with makeup artists and hair stylists.

thing about being a model, according to Rosario, is the pressure to look "close to perfect" all the time.[13]

A DAY IN THE LIFE OF A FASHION MODEL

Most models' daily routine includes exercising. Looking good and being healthy are important to getting work because of how competitive modeling is. Being fit and relaxed also makes models feel confident about their appearance. In addition, models need to eat a healthy diet and know how to maintain their weight.

Making and attending appointments is the biggest part of models' daily routine. To answer questions and learn about new work, models must be available throughout the day to take phone calls and respond to e-mails. They must also be available to attend "go-sees," fittings, and rehearsals. Because models might attend several appointments in one day, they need to be well groomed for wherever they might go. To be prepared, most models carry a small suitcase containing several wardrobe basics—for a woman, black pumps, leggings, and a strapless bra.

Many fashion models have other jobs, both to pursue other interests and to support themselves financially. A number of models also perform as actors and musicians. Whatever the job, it must be flexible enough to allow time to attend "go-sees" and bookings. Ideally, a model's part-time job will help with networking or making connections with people who will lead to bookings. Models can also make these connections by attending high-profile events such as local club openings and fundraisers.

TOP FIVE QUESTIONS ABOUT BECOMING A FASHION MODEL

1. *What can I do now to prepare myself for a career as a model?*

   Focus on getting experience as a performer and on becoming recognized for your looks and talents. For example, take dance classes, perform as an actor and a musician, and participate in talent shows and beauty pageants. Keep physically fit by playing a sport, and eat a healthy diet to maintain your weight. Learn about coordinating clothes, applying makeup, and styling hair by attending a modeling school or beauty school, if one is available.

2. *How can I get modeling jobs?*

   The best way to get modeling jobs is to sign with a talent or modeling agency.

3. *How much does it cost to get started?*

   Getting started should not cost you a lot of money. Reputable agencies don't charge new models a fee to sign with them, nor do they expect new models to submit professionally taken photographs. Requests for fees and expensive photos often indicate modeling scams.

4. *Can I start working as a fashion model right now?*

   It depends on how old you are. If you are at least 18 years old, you can start looking for agents on your

Models show off all kinds of clothing on the runway.

own. If you are under 18, you will probably need your parents' or guardians' permission to sign with an agent.[14]

5. *How much money will I make?*
    Although models have the potential to earn a lot of money, most of them don't. In 2009, the average US model made approximately $27,330 per year. The hourly fees for modeling in 2009 were approximately $17.51 per hour. But most models don't work every day, and many modeling jobs take only a few hours.[15]

A fashion model must have an understanding of how to move her body in a way that shows off the garment she is modeling.

WOULD YOU MAKE A GOOD FASHION MODEL?

When you think of what it takes to be a fashion model, the first word that comes to mind is probably *beauty*. In fact, having a certain type of physical appearance is the most important quality in fashion modeling. However, many more qualities are important, too.

LOOKING GOOD

High-fashion models tend to have unique faces and sometimes even exaggerated features. Although there are no absolute physical requirements for models, most clothing manufacturers look for models of certain ages, heights, and sizes. Women should be between 16 and 30 years old, from 5'8" (172.7 cm) to 5'11" (180.3 cm) in height, and between a 6 and a 10 in US dress size. Men should be in the same age group, from 6' (182.9 cm) to 6'2" (188.0 cm) in height, and a 40 or 42 regular in US clothing size.[1] If you don't fit these specifications, you might consider specialty modeling. After all, clothing and accessories are made for all ages,

CATEGORIES OF FASHION MODELS

Fashion models can be grouped into two categories:

1. Editorial models have unique facial features, such as huge eyes. They are often taller, thinner, and younger than other models. Because these individuals are so unusual in appearance, the general public views them as exotic. Editorial models are in demand for high-fashion work, so they tend to model clothes by famous fashion designers.

2. Commercial models have more classic features, such as a great smile, and are more traditional in terms of height, weight, and age. The general public views these models as friendly and approachable. Their mainstream appeal makes them well suited to a wide range of modeling work.

shapes, and sizes. Petite and plus-size clothing are examples of specialty areas that need models of different heights and sizes.

Perhaps most important in terms of appearance is photographing well. This involves more than being attractive. Being well groomed, for instance, is essential. In addition, models must take good care of their bodies. Having good posture and moving with grace and confidence are important, as well. Part of photographing well is looking natural and relaxed in front of the camera.

THE HIGH COST OF HIGH FASHION

Feeling pressure to be thin, some fashion models control their weight in unhealthy ways. A 2007 study by the Model Health Inquiry reported that up to 40 percent of models may have some kind of eating disorder.[2] The most well-known disorder is anorexia nervosa, in which a person drastically limits his or her intake of food. But among models, the most common disorder is probably bulimia, in which a person purges what he or she has eaten by vomiting or overusing laxatives.

FEELING GOOD

Modeling is a highly competitive business, so success in this career requires determination. Models must be able to take criticism and rejection without getting frustrated. And just as important, they must be willing to take direction and advice with a willing and positive attitude. Having strong communication skills and being patient helps models to interact well with agents, clients, and photographers.

Confidence is also key. Whether in front of a camera or an audience, models have to appear poised and self-assured. This can be difficult considering the unusual clothes models sometimes wear and the long, hard hours they often work.

Part of being confident comes from being healthy. Physical fitness is key not only to models' appearance but also to their endurance. Models spend hours at a time standing and walking, and they must sometimes sit or stand in uncomfortable poses. Having good control over their faces and bodies is needed to have the right expression or to hold a specific pose. Working out, eating well, and getting enough sleep all contribute to being fit.

CHECKLIST

Do you have what it takes to become a fashion model? To find out, answer these questions:

- *Do people often tell you that you are attractive?*

- *Do you meet the guidelines for age, height, and size?*

- *Do you photograph well?*

- *Do you have a strong sense of style?*

- *Are you strongly committed to the things you love to do?*

- *Are you confident and poised in front of people?*

- *Can you accept criticism and take advice?*

- *Are you healthy and physically fit?*

If you answered yes to all or most of these questions, a career in fashion modeling might be for you. Don't worry if you answered no to some of the questions. By working hard and finding a market for your specific look, you will have a chance to succeed in this field.

HOW TO GET THERE

GETTING THE MOST OUT OF HIGH SCHOOL

Having the proper education can be very important to a model. To prepare for a career as a model, choose useful courses in high school. Courses in drama, speech, and music will help you become confident in front of people. Courses in sewing and art will help you learn about clothes and fashion. To stay physically fit, participate in dance or other sports. While in high school, you might also complete a program at a beauty school or modeling school. There, you will learn how to apply makeup and style hair, how to choose flattering clothes, and how to walk and stand with confidence and poise.

GOING TO COLLEGE

Although having a college degree isn't required for being a model, you should consider getting one. More and more often, modeling and talent agencies prefer that their models have a college degree. These individuals usually have strong communication skills, as well as general knowledge about their culture and society. Suggested college courses for individuals interested in modeling include those in fashion

Dance, music, or acting classes can help develop the confidence and poise needed to be a model.

and art, drama and speech, and health and fitness. Basic business courses, such as accounting and marketing, are recommended as well.

GOING TO WORK

During high school and college, many future models work as sales associates in clothing stores. This early work experience helps them learn how clothes are constructed and how they should fit, as well as what looks good on different shapes and sizes of people.

Another benefit of working in a clothing store is having the chance to network with people in the fashion business.

Fashion buyers, sales associates, and display artists can provide useful information and insights about fashion. Some may even be able to provide important contacts for getting modeling jobs—for instance, at a local fashion show or shopping mall. Attending a beauty school or modeling school can provide similar networking benefits.

Most models start their careers in the city closest to where they live. They sign with a local modeling or talent agency, which finds them work at area stores, fashion shows, and special events. Building a portfolio, or book of photographs, that shows a range of modeling experience is important in getting started. After getting some local experience, successful models may move to a secondary market, such as Chicago, Dallas, or Atlanta. And with success at this level, a model might move to one of the world's fashion centers, such as New York City.

As you begin your career as a model, be careful not to be taken advantage of. There are many scams in which modeling

TYRA BANKS

The history of the modeling business is filled with stories of repeated rejection followed by tremendous success. One of the best examples is the story of supermodel Tyra Banks, host of *America's Next Top Model*. She was rejected by four modeling agencies before being signed by Elite Model Management at the age of 17. Soon after signing, she was singled out as the agency's only new model asked to go to Paris to walk the runway. Looking back, Banks said, "I didn't leave thinking I was going to be some big fashion model. I just wanted to make money for college."[3]

Tyra Banks was rejected by four modeling agencies before being signed.

agencies and photographers ask new models to pay high fees. Know what you should and should not have to pay for. Don't sign a contract or agreement without first having an agent or lawyer review it.

GET YOUR FOOT IN THE DOOR

Whatever fashion career you are interested in, start preparing for it now. Use school, community, and Internet resources to learn about fashion-related jobs in your area. For instance, contact an instructor in the art or design program at a local college. Explain that you are a student who's interested in learning more about the fashion industry, and ask for suggestions on whom to contact for information. Many instructors are willing to provide the names of individuals who have graduated from the college and are working for local employers.

Next, contact these individuals to arrange for informational interviews. Most people are quite willing to talk about their work and to give advice to students. If possible, conduct each interview face-to-face, so you can meet the individual. Doing so will result in a more personal interview and make a more lasting impression than talking over the phone or corresponding via e-mail. Also, ask about the possibility of spending the day with the interviewee, which is called job shadowing.

In addition, look for other ways to meet people in the fashion business. Volunteer with organizations that put on fashion shows and similar events, or get a part-time job at a clothing store or camera shop. Talk to fashion professionals not only about the different things they do but also what they like and don't like about their jobs. Also, ask what made them decide on their career. Take advantage of every opportunity to network.

As you meet people and get some hands-on experience, also work on developing your self-confidence. Try to push yourself beyond your current level of comfort by asking questions, making suggestions, and trying new things. Look for ways to make yourself stand out and be recognized. Finally, ask for feedback—good and bad—and learn to take criticism without becoming frustrated or defeated.

PROFESSIONAL ORGANIZATIONS

Here are some professional organizations that you might want to contact for more information about the jobs in this book.

CLOTHING DESIGNER

Council of Fashion Designers of America
www.cfda.com

Custom Tailors and Designers Association
www.ctda.com

International Association of Clothing Designers and Executives
www.iacde.net

National Association of Schools of Art and Design
nasad.arts-accredit.org

CLOTHING BUYER

American Purchasing Society
www.american-purchasing.com

Fashion Group International
www.fgi.org

Institute for Supply Management
www.ism.ws

National Retail Federation
www.nrffoundation.com

FASHION PHOTOGRAPHER

American Photographic Artists
www.apanational.com

American Society of Media Photographers
asmp.org

Editorial Photographers
www.editorialphoto.com

Professional Photographers of America
www.ppa.com

FASHION MODEL

International Modeling and Talent Association
www.imta.com

Modeling Association of America International
www.maai.org

North American Modeling Association
www.nama.ca

MARKET FACTS

JOB	NUMBER OF JOBS	GROWTH RATE	
Clothing Designer	15,780	little or no change	
Clothing Buyer	2,120	as fast as average	
Photographer	152,000	as fast as average	
Fashion Model	2,200	faster than average	

	ANNUAL MEDIAN WAGE	RELATED JOBS	SKILLS
	$64,260	*textile designer, accessory designer, floral designer*	*creative, artistic, proficient in sewing*
	$45,850	*sales representative, clothing designer, boutique owner*	*understanding of marketing, organized, good communication*
	$29,440	*creative director, graphic designer, artist*	*artistic, business minded, creative*
	$27,330	*specialty modeling work, actor, clothing designer, dancer*	*photogenic, confident, hardworking, adaptable*

All statistics from the *Bureau of Labor Statistics Occupational Outlook Handbook, 2010–2011 Edition*

GLOSSARY

boutique
A small store that specializes in a kind of merchandise, such as women's clothing.

collection
In fashion, an array of clothing created by a designer, usually for a specific season.

design house
The company or business of a fashion designer.

exclusive
Of limited or selected availability or use; not available to everyone.

fashion show
An event put on by a clothing designer to present his or her most recent fashions to buyers and the media.

fitting
The act of trying on clothes to have them adjusted to fit properly.

garment
An item of clothing.

high fashion
The latest trendsetting fashions by the world's top designers.

line
In fashion, the array of clothing created by a designer.

marketing
The process of developing, promoting, and selling products or services.

modeling agency
A company that represents models in business matters, arranging work for them in exchange for a percentage of their earnings.

portfolio
A collection of one's creative work that is shown to potential clients or employers.

retail
The selling of merchandise directly to consumers, usually in small amounts and at prices above cost.

sales associates
Individuals who sell merchandise in retail stores.

textiles
Fabrics.

trade show
An event at which the newest goods or services of a specific industry are displayed and promoted to potential buyers.

wholesale
The selling of merchandise to a retailer or distributor, usually in large amounts and at lower prices than are offered to consumers.

ADDITIONAL RESOURCES

FURTHER READINGS

Calderin, Jay. *Form, Fit, Fashion*. Beverly, MA: Rockport, 2009. Print.

Dickerson, Kitty G. *Inside the Fashion Business*. 7th ed. Upper Saddle River, NJ: Prentice-Hall, 2003. Print.

Goss, Judy. *Break into Modeling for Under $20*. New York: St. Martin's, 2008. Print.

Hartsog, Debbie. *Creative Careers in Fashion*. New York: Allsworth, 2007. Print.

J. G. Ferguson Publishing Company. *Ferguson's Careers in Focus: Fashion*. 3rd ed. New York: Infobase, 2007. Print.

Mauro, Lucia. *Careers for Fashion Plates and Other Trendsetters*. 2nd ed. Chicago: VGM Career, 2003. Print.

Polan, Brenda, and Roger Tredre. *The Great Fashion Designers*. Oxford: Berg, 2009. Print.

Press, Debbie. *Your Modeling Career: You Don't Have to Be a Superstar to Succeed*. New York: Allworth, 2003. Print.

Siegel, Eliot. *Fashion Photography Course*. New York: Quarto, 2008. Print.

Vogt, Peter. *Career Opportunities in the Fashion Industry*. New York: Checkmark, 2007. Print.

WEB LINKS

To learn more about fashion jobs, visit ABDO Publishing Company online at **www.abdopublishing.com**. Web sites about fashion jobs are featured on our Book Links page. These links are routinely monitored and updated to provide the most current information available.

SOURCE NOTES

CHAPTER 1. IS A FASHION JOB FOR YOU?

1. Karen Karbo. *The Gospel According to Coco Chanel: Life Lessons from the World's Most Elegant Woman*. Guilford, CT: Globe Pequot, 2009. Print. 221.

2. Linda Ames. "The Little Black Dress." *Vintage Textile*. Linda Ames, n.d. Web. 19 June 2010.

3. Fiona Valentine. "Edith Head." *Film Reference*. Advameg, Inc., 2010. Web. 5 Aug. 2010.

4. Nikki Katz. *The Everything Cryptograms Books*. Avon, MA: F+W, 2005. Print. 29.

5. Robert McG. Thomas Jr. "Gene Moore, 88, Window Display Artist, Dies." *New York Times*. New York Times, 26 Nov. 1998. Web. 9 July 2010.

6. Christopher Hopkins. *Staging Your Comeback: A Complete Beauty Revival for Women Over 45*. Deerfield Beach, FL: Health Communications, 2008. Print. 78.

CHAPTER 2. WHAT IS A CLOTHING DESIGNER?

1. Lucia Mauro. *Careers for Fashion Plates and Other Trendsetters*. 2nd ed. Chicago: VGM Career, 2003. Print. 14.

2. U.S. Bureau of Labor Statistics. "Fashion Designers." *Occupational Outlook Handbook, 2010-11 Edition*. U.S. Bureau of Labor Statistics, 17 Dec. 2009. Web. 11 July 2010.

3. J. G. Ferguson Publishing Company. *Ferguson's Careers in Focus: Fashion*. New York: Infobase, 2007. Print. 66.

4. "Haute Couture." *Merriam-Webster.com*. Merriam-Webster, Inc., 2010. Web. 26 Jul. 2010.

5. U.S. Bureau of Labor Statistics. "Fashion Designers." *Occupational Outlook Handbook, 2010-11 Edition*. U.S. Bureau of Labor Statistics, 17 Dec. 2009. Web. 11 July 2010.

6. Nina Callaway. "Who Is Vera Wang?" *About.com*. About.com, n.d. Web. 26 July 2010.

7. Nina Callaway. "What Do Wedding Dresses Cost?" *About.com*. About.com, n.d. Web. 26 July 2010.

8. U.S. Bureau of Labor Statistics. "Fashion Designers." *Occupational Outlook Handbook, 2010-11 Edition*. U.S. Bureau of Labor Statistics, 17 Dec. 2009. Web. 11 July 2010.

9. Debbie Hartsog. *Creative Careers in Fashion*. New York: Allsworth, 2007. Print. 15.

10. Wayne Laberda. Message to the author. 4 Aug. 2010. E-mail.

11. Ibid.

12. Ibid.

13. Ibid.

14. U.S. Bureau of Labor Statistics. "Fashion Designers." *Occupational Outlook Handbook, 2010-11 Edition*. U.S. Bureau of Labor Statistics, 17 Dec. 2009. Web. 11 July 2010.

CHAPTER 3. WOULD YOU MAKE A GOOD CLOTHING DESIGNER?

1. "Ralph Lauren: Fashion Designer." *fashion.infomat*. InfoMat, Inc., 18 Jan. 2007. Web. 5 Aug. 2010.

2. Lucia Mauro. *Careers for Fashion Plates and Other Trendsetters*. Chicago: VGM Career, 2003. Print. 19.

3. "About FIT." *Fashion Institute of Technology*. Fashion Institute of Technology, n.d. Web. 30 July 2010.

4. "About Parsons." *Parsons*. Parsons, The New School, n.d. Web. 30 July 2010.

5. "Domenico Dolce: Fashion Designer." *fashion.infomat*. InfoMat, Inc., 18 Jan. 2007. Web. 5 Aug. 2010.

CHAPTER 4. WHAT IS A CLOTHING BUYER?

1. Mike Sachoff. "U.S. Online Retail Set for Double-Digit Growth." *WebProNews*. iEntry Network, 8 Mar. 2010. Web. 10 Aug. 2010.

2. U.S. Bureau of Labor Statistics. "Wholesale and Retail Buyers, Except Farm Products." *Occupational Outlook Handbook, 2010-11 Edition*. U.S. Bureau of Labor Statistics, May 2009. Web. 25 July 2010.

3. Ibid.

4. Maggie Mullen. Message to the author. 9 Aug. 2010. E-mail.

5. Ibid.

6. Ibid.

CHAPTER 5. WOULD YOU MAKE A GOOD CLOTHING BUYER?

1. J. D. Power and Associates. "JCPenney, Kohl's, Macy's, Neiman Marcus and Nordstrom Lead Department Store Customer Satisfaction Rankings." *PRNewswire*. PR Newswire Association, LLC, 11 Oct. 2007. Web. 8 Aug. 2010.

SOURCE NOTES CONTINUED

CHAPTER 6. WHAT IS A FASHION PHOTOGRAPHER?

1. J. G. Ferguson Publishing Company. *Ferguson's Careers in Focus: Fashion.* New York: Infobase, 2007. Print. 96.

2. U.S. Bureau of Labor Statistics. "Photographers." *Occupational Outlook Handbook, 2010-11 Edition.* U.S. Bureau of Labor Statistics, 17 Dec. 2009. Web. 25 July 2010.

3. J. G. Ferguson Publishing Company. *Ferguson's Careers in Focus: Fashion.* New York: Infobase, 2007. Print. 97.

4. "Starting Your Fashion Photographer Career." *AllArtSchools.* All Star Directories, Inc., n.d. Web. 12 Aug. 2010.

5. Ramon Moreno. Message to the author. 12 Aug. 2010. E-mail.

6. Ibid.

7. Ibid.

8. Ibid.

9. "Online Shopping." *National Camera Exchange & Video.* National Camera Exchange & Video, 2010. Web. 12 Aug. 2010.

10. Ramon Moreno. Message to the author. 12 Aug. 2010. E-mail.

11. U.S. Bureau of Labor Statistics. "Occupational Employment and Wages, May 2009." *Occupational Outlook Handbook, 2010-11 Edition.* U.S. Bureau of Labor Statistics, 14 May. 2010. Web. 25 July 2010.

CHAPTER 7. WOULD YOU MAKE A GOOD FASHION PHOTOGRAPHER?

1. Ramon Moreno. Message to the author. 12 Aug. 2010. E-mail.

2. "About PPA" *PPA: Professional Photographers of America.* Professional Photographers of America, n.d. Web. 12 Aug. 2010.

CHAPTER 8. WHAT IS A FASHION MODEL?

1. U.S. Bureau of Labor Statistics. "Models." *Occupational Outlook Handbook, 2010-11 Edition.* U.S. Bureau of Labor Statistics, 17 Dec. 2009. Web. 25 July 2010.

2. Judy Goss. *Breaking into Modeling for Under $20.* New York: St. Martin's Griffin, 2008. Print. 11.

3. Lucia Mauro. *Careers for Fashion Plates and Other Trendsetters.* Chicago: VGM Career, 2003. Print. 103-104.

4. "Modeling Jobs." *JobMonkey.com*. JobMonkey, Inc., n.d. Web. 10 July 2010.

5. Lucia Mauro. *Careers for Fashion Plates and Other Trendsetters*. Chicago: VGM Career, 2003. Print. 104.

6. U.S. Bureau of Labor Statistics. "Models." *Occupational Outlook Handbook, 2010-11 Edition*. U.S. Bureau of Labor Statistics, 17 Dec. 2009. Web. 25 July 2010.

7. Tearra Rosario. Message to the author. 25 July 2010. E-mail.

8. Ibid.

9. Ibid.

10. Ibid.

11. Tearra Rosario. Message to the author. 25 July 2010. E-mail.

12. "Male Modeling Not Glamorous or Lucrative. At All." *New York*. New York Magazine, 3 Mar. 2009. Web. 10 July 2010.

13. Tearra Rosario. Message to the author. 25 July 2010. E-mail.

14. "Be Discovered." *elitemodel.com*. elite, n.d. Web. 29 Sept. 2010.

15. U.S. Bureau of Labor Statistics. "Models." *Occupational Outlook Handbook, 2010-11 Edition*. U.S. Bureau of Labor Statistics, 14 May 2010. Web. 25 July 2010.

CHAPTER 9. WOULD YOU MAKE A GOOD FASHION MODEL?

1. J. G. Ferguson Publishing Company. *Ferguson's Careers in Focus: Fashion*. New York: Infobase, 2007. Print. 146.

2. Christian Nordqvist. "Eating Disorders among Fashion Models Rising." *Medical News Today*. MediLexicon International Ltd., 8 July 2007. Web. 5 Aug. 2010.

3. Marcellous L. Jones. "Tyra Banks." *Fashion Insider*. Fashion Insider, n.d. Web. 5 Aug. 2010.

INDEX

ABOUT THE AUTHOR

Susan M. Freese, a freelance writer and editor, holds B.A. and M.A. degrees in English. During her 27-year career, she has developed and produced educational materials for students of many levels. She has also taught college-level literature, writing, and communication courses. Susan's interest in music and the arts has involved her in writing promotional and grant materials for several nonprofit organizations, including the Medalist Fine Arts Association and the Bloomington Fine Arts Council. She is also the current president of the Minnesota Bookbuilders, a group of professionals who work in various facets of producing books. Susan lives in Minneapolis, Minnesota.

PHOTO CREDITS